FACT CAT

MATERIALS

Izzi Howell

WAYLAND
www.waylandbooks.co.uk

FACT CAT

Get your paws on this fantastic new mega-series from Wayland!

Join our Fact Cat on a journey of fun learning about every subject under the sun!

Published in Great Britain in 2018 by Wayland
Copyright © Wayland 2016

ISBN: 9781526301710
10 9 8 7 6 5 4 3 2 1

MIX
Paper from responsible sources
FSC® C104740

Wayland
An imprint of Hachette Children's Group
Part of Hodder & Stoughton
Carmelite House
50 Victoria Embankment
London EC4Y 0DZ

An Hachette UK Company
www.hachette.co.uk
www.hachettechildrens.co.uk

A catalogue for this title is available from
the British Library
Printed and bound in China

Produced for Wayland by
White-Thomson Publishing Ltd
www.wtpub.co.uk

Editor: Izzi Howell
Design: Clare Nicholas
Fact Cat illustrations: Shutterstock/Julien Troneur
Consultant: Karina Philip

Picture and illustration credits:
iStock: piotr_malczyk cover, EVAfotografie 5l, vm 10, Elenathewise 18; Shutterstock: StacieStauffSmith Photos title page and 14, Hogan Imaging 4, windu 5r, SOMMAI 6l, Africa Studio 6c, OlegDoroshin 6r, yongyut rukkachatsuwa 7, subin pumsom 8, AS Food studio 9t, bdstudio 9b, photka 11, Inga Nielsen 12, MikeBiTa 13, Hurst Photo 15l, design56 15c, TinnaPong 15r, UMB-O 16, Dasha Petrenko 17, Elnur 19l, Mariusz Szczygiel 19r, XiXinXing 20, Sergey Maksimov 21.

Every effort has been made to clear copyright.
Should there be any inadvertent omission,
please apply to the publisher for rectification.

The author, Izzi Howell, is a writer and editor specialising in children's educational publishing.

The consultant, Karina Philip, is a teacher and a primary literacy consultant with an MA in creative writing.

FACT CAT FACT

There is a question for you to answer on every spread in this book. You can check your answers on page 24.

CONTENTS

WHAT IS A MATERIAL?

We use materials, such as wood, plastic and metal, to make different objects. A book is made from paper. A blanket is made from wool.

cotton

plastic

Some objects are made from more than one material. This boy's shirt is made from cotton (fabric) and plastic (buttons). Which materials are jeans made from?

Each material has different **properties**. These are the words that we use to describe a material. For example, glass is hard and smooth.

A **ceramic** plate feels hard, but it is not strong. It will break easily if you drop it.

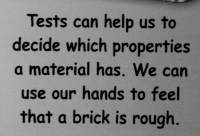

Tests can help us to decide which properties a material has. We can use our hands to feel that a brick is rough.

FACT CAT **FACT**

Some materials have different properties, depending on how they have been treated. When wood is cut from a tree, it feels rough. However, if you rub wood with **sandpaper**, it becomes smooth.

SOLIDS, LIQUIDS AND GASES

Materials can be **solids**, **liquids** or **gases**. Solid materials keep their shape. Liquids can flow into the shape of any container you put them in. Gases float in the air.

Water can be a solid, a liquid or a gas, depending on its temperature.

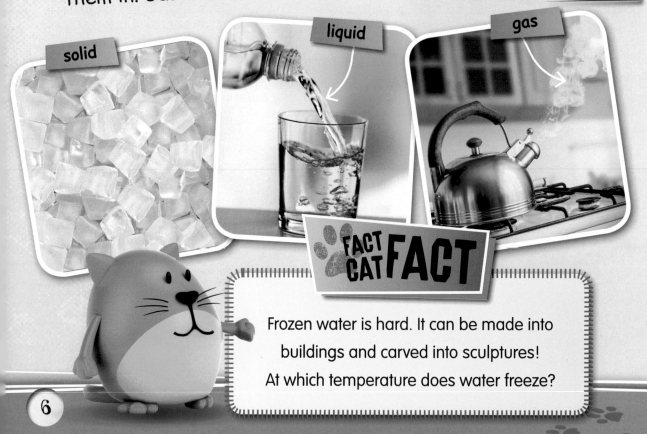

solid

liquid

gas

FACT CAT FACT

Frozen water is hard. It can be made into buildings and carved into sculptures! At which temperature does water freeze?

Metal and plastic are solid at **room temperature**. However, if you heat them to a very high temperature, they will **melt** into liquids. When they cool down, they will become solids again.

This liquid metal is being poured into a round container. When the metal cools down, it will become solid and have a round shape, like the container.

CHOOSING A MATERIAL

When you are making an object, it is important to choose a material that has the right properties. For example, an object that needs to be hard, such as a knife, should be made from a hard material, such as metal.

A chair needs to be made from a strong material, such as wood, so that it can hold the weight of the person sitting on it.

FACT CAT FACT

Diamonds are one of the hardest materials on Earth. Diamond tools are often used to cut through other materials.

Objects made from the wrong material will break easily or will not be useful. For example, rock is too hard and **rigid** to be made into clothes.

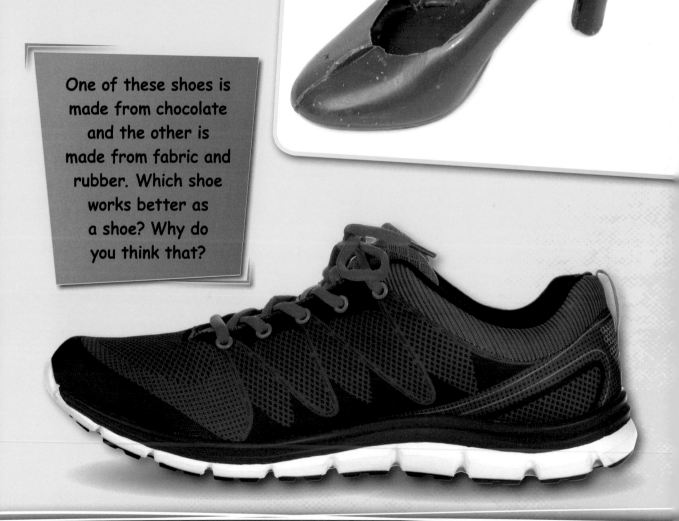

One of these shoes is made from chocolate and the other is made from fabric and rubber. Which shoe works better as a shoe? Why do you think that?

FINDING MATERIALS

Some materials come straight from nature. Wood comes from the trunks and thick branches of trees. Rock is dug out of the ground in **quarries**.

You need a strong metal tool, such as an electric chainsaw, to cut down trees to get wood.

People can make natural materials into new, **man-made** materials. Paper is made from wood. Fabric is made from threads that have been **woven** together.

Plastic is a man-made material. It is made from thick, black oil that is found deep underground. Can plastic be turned back into oil?

FACT CAT FACT

Glass is made from sand! When the sand is heated to a very high temperature, it melts into a liquid. When the liquid cools down, it forms glass.

CHANGING SHAPE

Forces affect each material in a different way. We can change the shape of some solid materials by bending them or twisting them.

If you bend aluminium foil, it will keep its new shape. That makes it a good material for wrapping around other objects, such as these potatoes.

FACT CAT FACT

Used aluminium cans and tins can be melted down and made into new containers. It only takes around 60 days for an aluminium can to be **recycled**.

Rubber is a stretchy material. If you push or pull rubber, it will change its shape. However, it will go back to its original shape if you stop pulling or pushing it.

When the girl sits on the rubber ball, the ball is squashed by her weight. What will happen to the shape of the ball if the girl stands up?

MATERIALS AND LIGHT

Some types of metal, plastic and glass are shiny. When light hits a shiny material, the light is **reflected** off its **surface**.

These ornaments are made from shiny plastic. What is the opposite of shiny?

We can see through **transparent** materials because they let light pass through them. **Translucent** materials only let a little light through, so you cannot see through them very clearly.

Plastic can be transparent, translucent or **opaque** (say oh-payk). You cannot see through opaque materials.

transparent

translucent

opaque

FACT CAT FACT

When a light shines on translucent or opaque material, the material blocks the light and a shadow is formed.

WATER

Materials act in different ways when you put them in water. Some materials, such as paper, **absorb** the water and become wet.

This boy is drying his hair with a towel after a shower. The fabric towel absorbs the water.

Waterproof materials do not absorb water. The water sits on the surface of the object or falls away easily.

Wellington boots are made out of rubber, a waterproof material. Name another waterproof object that you use in the rain and the material that it is made from.

FACT CAT FACT

Birds that spend a lot of time in water make their feathers waterproof so that they don't feel wet and cold! They do this by spreading their feathers with special oil that they make themselves.

ELECTRICITY

Electricity can pass through some materials, such as the metals copper and iron. These materials are called electrical **conductors**. They are used in electrical cables and plugs.

When a metal cable is plugged into an electrical **socket**, electricity from the plug travels along the metal to power the lightbulb.

Most materials do not let electricity pass through them. They are called electrical **insulators**. Plastic, wood and glass are examples of electrical insulators.

plug

We wrap metal cables in plastic so that the electricity cannot escape. Why don't we wrap metal cables in wood or glass?

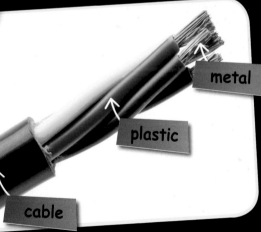

metal

plastic

cable

HEAT

Some materials, such as fabric and wood, are insulators of heat. They do not let heat pass through them.

Fabric hats and scarves keep you warm in the cold. This is because they stop the heat from your body escaping.

Heat moves easily through some materials, such as the metals steel and aluminium. These materials are good conductors of heat.

Pans need to be made from a material that conducts heat. This is so that the food inside the pan heats up and cooks quickly.

plastic

metal

FACT CAT FACT

Saucepans often have plastic handles so that you don't burn your hands on the hot metal. Is plastic an insulator or a conductor of heat?

Try to answer the questions below.
Look back through the book to help
you. Check your answers on page 24.

1 Which of these
is a property of glass?

a) bendy

b) smooth

c) absorbent

2 Metal is a liquid
at room temperature.
True or not true?

a) true

b) not true

3 Plastic is a man-made
material. True or not true?

a) true

b) not true

4 Which word describes
a material that light cannot
pass through?

a) transparent

b) translucent

c) opaque

5 Fabric absorbs water.
True or not true?

a) true

b) not true

6 Which material isn't
an electrical insulator?

a) plastic

b) copper

c) wood

GLOSSARY

absorb to take something in

ceramic made from clay that has been baked

conductor something that lets electricity or heat pass through

force a push or a pull

gas something that is neither a solid nor a liquid, such as air

insulator something that does not let electricity or heat pass through

liquid something that is neither a solid nor a gas, such as milk

man-made describes something that has been made by humans

melt to turn from a solid to a liquid

opaque describes something that does not let light through

property a characteristic of something, such as hard, smooth or transparent

quarry a place where rock and sand are dug out of the ground

recycled when an old product is turned into a new product

reflect if something reflects light, it sends the light back and does not absorb it

rigid describes something that is not able to be bent

room temperature the temperature inside a normal building that isn't too hot or too cold

sandpaper paper with a rough surface that is rubbed against wood to make it smooth

socket the place in the wall where you can connect a cable to the electrical supply

solid something that is neither a liquid nor a gas, such as a table

surface the top part of something

translucent describes something that some light can pass through

transparent describes something that you can see through

waterproof describes something that does not let water through

woven describes a cloth that is made by threads that have been crossed over each other

INDEX

ANSWERS

Pages 4–21

Page 4: Jeans are made from cotton and metal (buttons/zip).

Page 6: 0 degrees Celsius

Page 9: The fabric and rubber shoe would be better, because chocolate breaks easily.

Page 11: No, it cannot be made back into oil.

Page 13: The ball will go back to its original shape.

Page 14: Dull

Page 17: Some options include raincoat or umbrella, both of which are made from plastic.

Page 19: Because they are not bendy.

Page 21: Insulator

Quiz answers

1   b – smooth

2   not true – it is a solid at room temperature and only melts at very high temperatures.

3   true

4   c – opaque

5   true

6   b – copper